The 3 minute workbook®

43 creative exercises for

Managing With Coaching

*Micro workouts,
Macro changes.*

 Self awareness   Championing

 Listening   Feedback

 Challenging   Goal setting

Kartik Bharadia

First published in Great Britain in 2024
ISBN: 9798878212199

Published by The 3 minute workbook®

Copyright © 2024 Kartik Bharadia

The rights of the author as identified in this work have been asserted by them in accordance with the Copyright, Designs and Patents Act 1988. Any pictures, images, annotations, or diagrams constitute an extension of the work asserted under the Copyright, Designs and Patents Act 1988.

All rights are reserved by The 3 minute workbook. No part of this publication may be reproduced, stored in or introduced into a retrieval system, or transmitted, in any form, including but not limited to electronic, mechanical, photocopying, or recording form without the prior written permission of The 3 minute workbook, except as permitted by the Copyright, Designs and Patents Act 1988. Anyone in breach of this disclaimer shall be liable for a civil claim in damages. For the avoidance of any doubt, the work produced by The 3 minute workbook are for educational purposes only.

Although we have made every effort to ensure that the information in this book was correct at press time, we do not assume and hereby disclaim any liability to any party for any loss (including consequential loss), damage, or disruption caused by errors or omissions, whether such errors or omissions result from negligence, negligent misrepresentation, accident, misinformation, factually incorrect information or any other cause. The author holds an honest opinion in their work. The works contained in this book are for educational purposes only and not the official position of The 3 minute workbook.

THE MAGIC OF 3 MINUTE WORKBOOKS

Most of us come across grand ideas but only few make it a reality. THE 3 MINUTE WORKBOOK is on a mission to increase the number of people living their desired reality by getting you implementing change with smaller goals that can be executed in 3 minutes. Secondly, every exercise is creatively minded to bring forth your personality and pace. Small but regular wins, will make you more courageous at approaching your big vision.

WHY THIS WORKBOOK?

Leadership is changing fast. With growing access to information, choice of opportunities, and transparency, employers and managers are more vested in nurturing their colleagues. Coaching has become the hallmark of supportive leadership that produces self aware, cooperative and self regulating thinkers. For businesses and organisations, coaching is proving to foster a more productive workforce, improving retention and contributing to innovation and success. In his landmark paper, 'Leadership that gets results' (Harvard Business Review, 2000), Daniel Goleman shares *"coaching leaders develop people for the future."*

It is seemingly not enough for leaders to rely solely on traditional management and leadership skills in a multigenerational, diverse and increasingly complex workspace. Leaders must adapt, be creative, and show empathy where effects of socioeconomics, race, gender, human rights and purpose are evident and intertwined.

Earlier generations are familiar with inflexible leadership who commanded with predominantly directive or pacesetting styles. Coaching practices in particular empower individuals to own and lead their workflow, development, goals and environment.

THE 3 MINUTE WORKBOOK for Leading With Coaching shares 40 plus timeless secrets so that you, your organisation and team can grow simultaneously, rapidly and without diluting individuality.

Dedicated to everyone who finds purpose in the pulls and pushes, daily.

CREATIVE STRATEGY

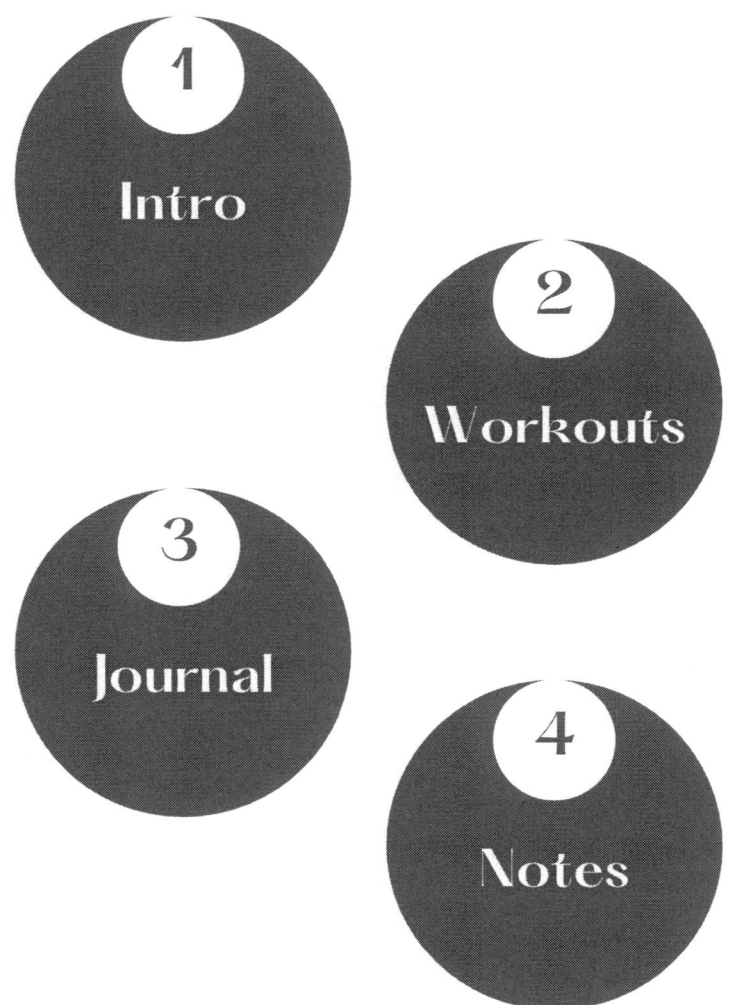

The 3 minute workbook

INTRODUCTION

"Who is a coach?" I can recall being one of the opening questions from our qualified instructor who was to steer a group of business leaders through a formal development programme. You can liken our coach's definition to the list of intended learning outcomes she set out for us. This included developing our wisdom and skills of self awareness, listening actively, challenging, championing and giving feedback effectively and setting clear goals. Much of the leadership course leaned on appreciating and applying models to hone in each coaching capability.

- **Self awareness** is fundamental for both the coach and coachee to realise potential within. A less recognised aspect of self awareness is how you think you project yourself and how you are being received.

- **Listening** is an art that requires constant review. As you habituate, learn or master a task, process or a space, achievement and ego in particular muddy this capability.

- **Challenging** is the sensibility of setting up an acknowledged benchmark and then with reference to this agreement holding to account for expansion in thought, action and ambition.

- **Championing** strives to seek opportunities to reinforce, recognise and encourage growth.

- **Feedback** when coaching is constructive and conducted without bias and avoidance of difficult conversations when necessary.

- **Goal setting** seeks to explore, stretch and bring forth a realistic view of the required commitments to action and review progress.

WHAT IS REQUIRED

The coaching style is conducive of discovering potential. This style of leadership will uncover new and sustain capabilities of organisations, teams, projects around you and of course, within you.

THE 3 MINUTE WORKBOOK was designed for you operate out of consistently rather than a one off training manual. Like a spoken language, the skill of coaching can be gained and forgotten and awkward in practice if it is under utilised. **Experimentation and regular application** of a wide range of coaching models will attain wholesome results.

Secondly, coaching is not a one style fits all when it comes to which exercise you use, with whom and upon any situation. It requires **constant judgement** to channel through the best leadership style or blend of styles, which may not involve coaching at all. Aptly, the workouts in this workbook promise to furnish you with more awareness and new leadership capabilities.

A linear exploration of this workbook is not required, although possible. The user is free to jump and loop through the coaching workouts as necessary. The skills key provided below utilises an icon for each of the **6 core coaching skills** being explored. Each exercise exhibits a dominant coaching skill which if habituated, can be mastered. The relevant icon will appear on the content page as well as the respective workout page.

To optimise the impact of each model, on the description page, look out for recommendations on the **'next suggested workouts'** which can easily be located in conjunction with the contents page.

Skills key

 Self awareness    Championing

 Listening    Feedback

 Challenging    Goal setting

COACHING WORKOUTS

Skill

01	A WHEEL OF LIFE	Page 16
02	ACTION PRIORITY	Page 18
03	CHANGE CURVE	Page 20
04	CHOICE MATTERS	Page 22
05	CIRCLES OF INFLUENCE	Page 24
06	EXTREME USER INTERVIEWS	Page 26
07	FEEDBACK MATRIX	Page 28
08	FISHBONE DIAGRAM	Page 30
09	FIVE WHYS	Page 32
10	FREE WRITTING	Page 34
11	GET IN THE ZONE	Page 36
12	INDEPENDENT OBSERVERS	Page 38
13	INSIGHTFUL ARTIST	Page 40
14	KINDNESS BINGO	Page 42
15	LEADERSHIP STYLE	Page 44

COACHING WORKOUTS

Skill

16	LIFE MAP	Page 46
17	LONG-RANGE FORECAST	Page 48
18	NIRVANA LETTER	Page 50
19	NOW WHAT	Page 52
20	NUDGE	Page 54
21	ODD DAY	Page 56
22	PASSION DRIVERS	Page 58
23	PITCH MATRIX	Page 60
24	PREDICT A HEADLINE	Page 62
25	PROJECTIONS	Page 64
26	REGULATE, RELATE, REASON	Page 66
27	REVERSE THINKING	Page 68
28	SCALING	Page 70
29	SCREENPLAY	Page 72
30	SELF APPRAISAL MATRIX	Page 74

COACHING WORKOUTS

			Skill
31	SOCIAL COGNITIVE THEORY	Page 76	💡
32	STATE MANAGEMENT	Page 78	🏯
33	SWOT MATRIX	Page 80	🎯
34	TGROW	Page 82	🏯
35	THE SMART MODEL	Page 84	🎯
36	THE 4 7 8 4	Page 86	👂
37	TIME-LAPSE VIDEO	Page 88	👂
38	USER STORY	Page 90	🎯
39	VIEW IT AGAIN	Page 92	👂
40	VISION BOARD	Page 94	🎯
41	WHEEL OF WORK	Page 96	💡
42	ZERO DRAFT	Page 98	🎯
43	3 MINUTE JOURNAL	Page 100	💡

A WHEEL OF LIFE

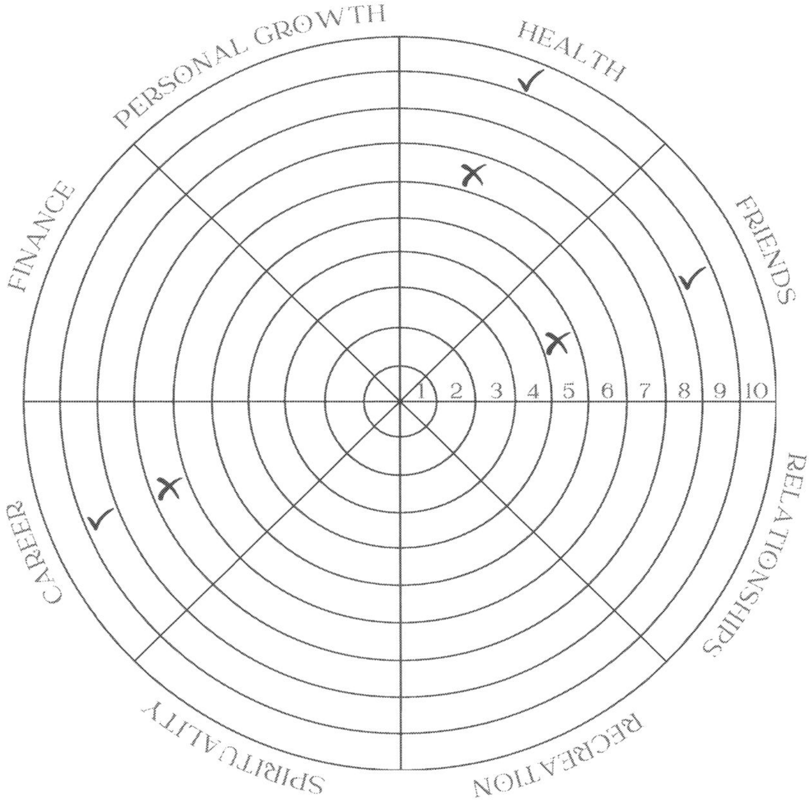

A concept originally created by Paul J. Meyer.

The 3 minute workbook

A WHEEL OF LIFE

First, find a blank piece of paper and draw a circle with 8 sections. Then, record 8 life domains that are important to you in each section. Now, as a measure of how much time you currently devote to each area, rate them 1 – 10 (high). Now for each, rate the ideal time to be devoted 1 – 10 (high) to yield growth in that domain. Finally, commit to a change plan for your 3 most important life priorities.

Next suggested workouts
2, 12, 30, 35, 40

Why?

Different areas of your life will need different levels of attention at different times.

ACTION PRIORITY

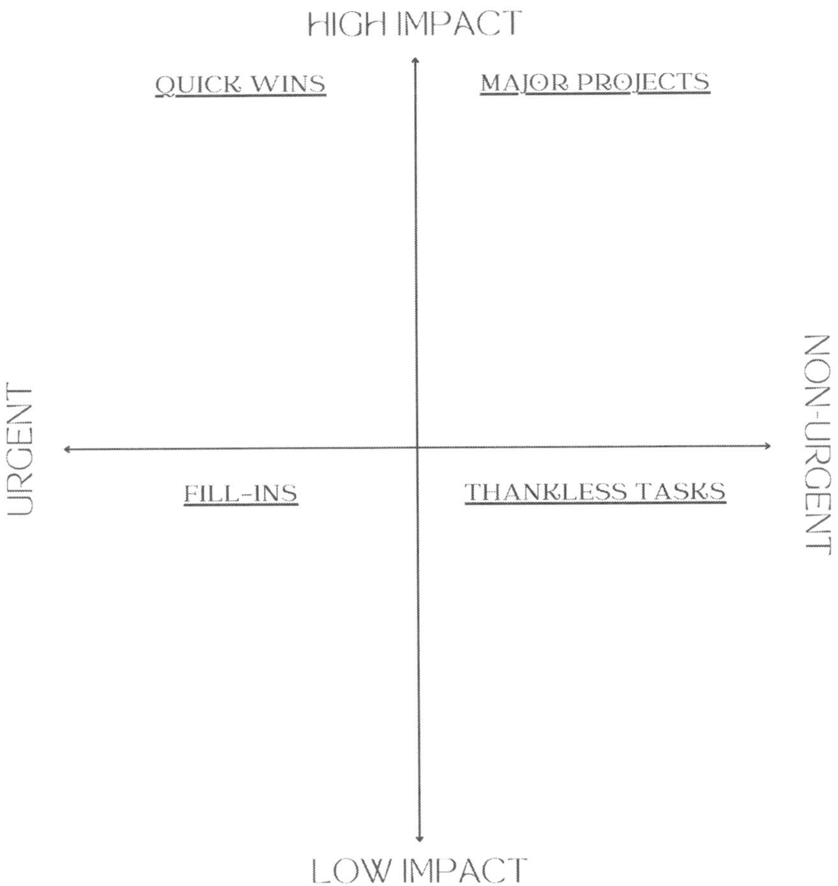

```
                    HIGH IMPACT
                         ↑
      QUICK WINS         |    MAJOR PROJECTS
                         |
                         |
  URGENT ────────────────┼──────────────── NON-URGENT
                         |
      FILL-INS           |    THANKLESS TASKS
                         |
                         ↓
                    LOW IMPACT
```

A concept explored by Stephen Covey, 7 habits of highly effective people (1991).

The 3 minute workbook

ACTION PRIORITY

List in total 8 current, medium or long term priorities that you value and contribute to your success.

Then, label each as 'urgent' or 'non-urgent'. Secondly, label each as 'high' or 'low' impact to your success.

Finally, place the priorities in the respective quadrants in terms of urgency versus impact. Then, evaluate.

Next suggested workouts
1, 14, 19, 30, 33, 35

Why?

A great way to visualise high impact but non urgent priorities (major projects), which often get neglected.

CHANGE CURVE

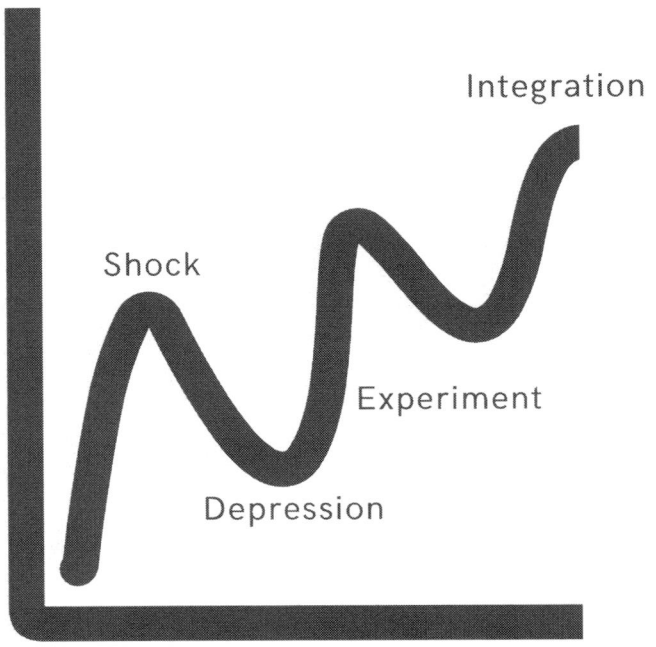

Elizabeth Kubler-Ross proposed the change curve in 1969.

The 3 minute workbook

CHANGE CURVE

Schedule a catch up with a new joinee or someone owning a novel project to share the Kubler-Ross change curve.

Ask about the changes they are expecting, those that may deplete their morale and their expectations of support. Then, agree a reasonable follow up to check in again.

Why?

A quick way to recognise the four stages in change are often accompanied by a range of emotions. Determine how best to support individuals throughout each stage.

Next suggested workouts
4, 5, 11, 27, 28, 30

CHOICE MATTERS

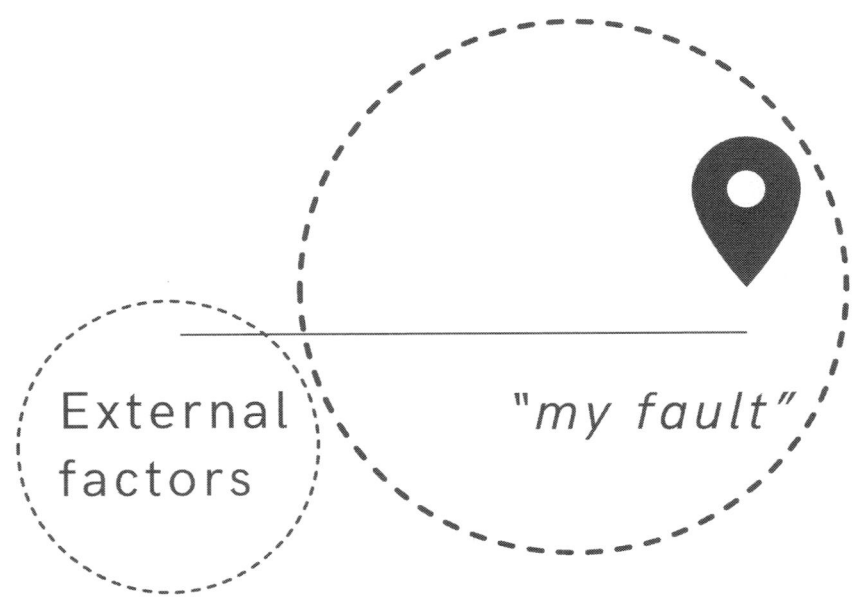

Others

Circumstances

Government

Health

CHOICE MATTERS

Take responsibility for your choices.

Set out 3 ways you will make this your day.

Why?

Next suggested workouts
1, 2, 32, 42, 43

A growth mindset fosters willingness to learn, adapt, and improve which, expands your internal locus of control. Be less controlled by external factors.

CIRCLES OF INFLUENCE

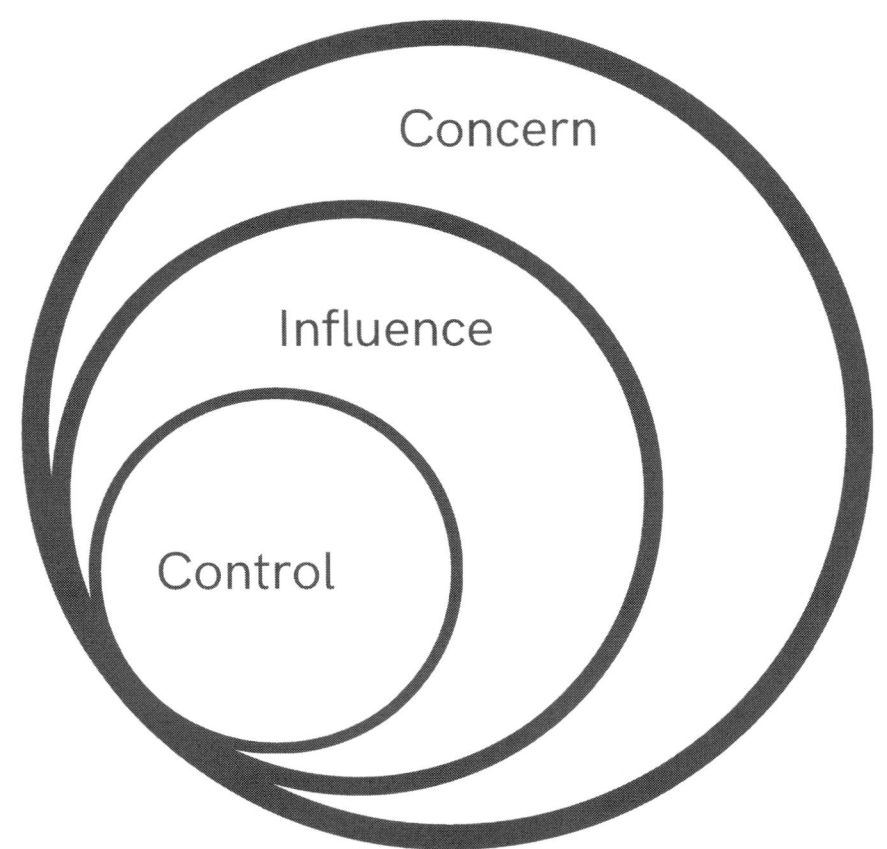

The 3 minute workbook

CIRCLES OF INFLUENCE

Fill in the three circles of influence with a list of factors that affect your life. Circle of control contains everything that you can have a direct impact upon. Circle of influence contains all that you are able to affect but not directly control. Circle of concern is the largest and contains everything that you might be concerned about but cannot control or influence. Finally, evaluate.

Why?

Next suggested workouts
2, 11, 14, 18, 40

A useful way to focus on areas of direct control or influence.

EXTREME USER INTERVIEWS

The 3 minute workbook

EXTREME USER INTERVIEWS

Get on the move and put on some new shoes to see things differently.

Ask very familiar or completely unfamiliar individuals to evaluate something you will work on or have worked on.

Why?

Next suggested workouts
9, 23, 34, 35, 40, 42

A quick and realistic way to avoid blind spots and to find improvements.

FEEDBACK MATRIX

WHAT I REALLY VALUE ABOUT YOU IS...	WHAT I WOULD ASK YOU TO START DOING/ DO MORE OF IS...
AND THE IMPACT THIS HAS ON ME IS...	AND THE IMPACT ON ME WOULD BE...
WHAT I WOULD ASK YOU TO STOP DOING IS...	BECAUSE I WANT YOU TO BE AT YOUR VERY BEST...
AND THE IMPACT ON ME WOULD BE...	THE ONE BEHAVIOR I WOULD ASK YOU TO WORK ON WOULD BE...

A coaching framework adapted by Matthew Radley & associates.

The 3 minute workbook

FEEDBACK MATRIX

Consider an individual you value. It may be a colleague, friend or client.

Use the feedback matrix to bring out their best. Write down your model feedback statement that adopts features from all four quadrants.

Why?

Next suggested workouts
11, 23, 28, 30, 34, 35

A constructive and focused way of promoting growth. Feedback should only refer to your experiences of the individual.

FISHBONE DIAGRAM

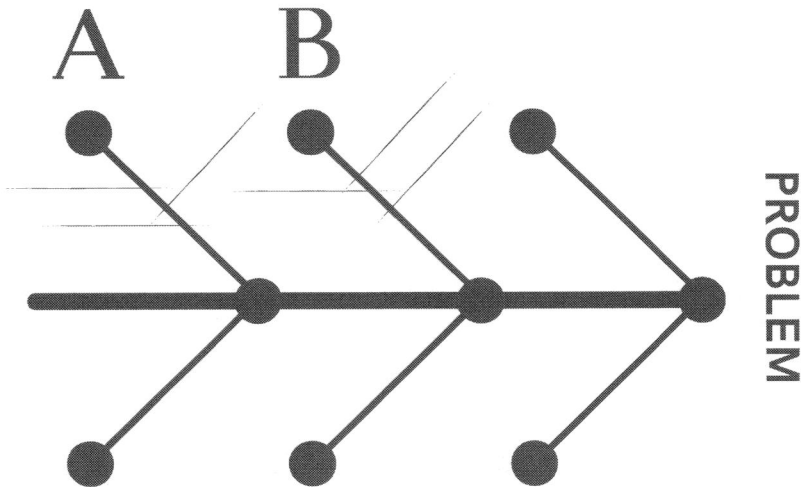

The fishbone diagram is created by Kaoru Ishikawa

FISHBONE DIAGRAM

Identify a major problem. Draw four or more branches off the large central arrow pointing to the problem. Each branch/ bone represents main categories of potential underlying factors and label each line.

Now, take each main categories and identify new bones contributing to this issue. Continue this for every new bone. Finally, evaluate the diagram.

Why?

Next suggested workouts
11, 19, 22, 34, 35

Useful exercise to identify a wider range of possible underlying factors — not just the most obvious.

FIVE WHYS

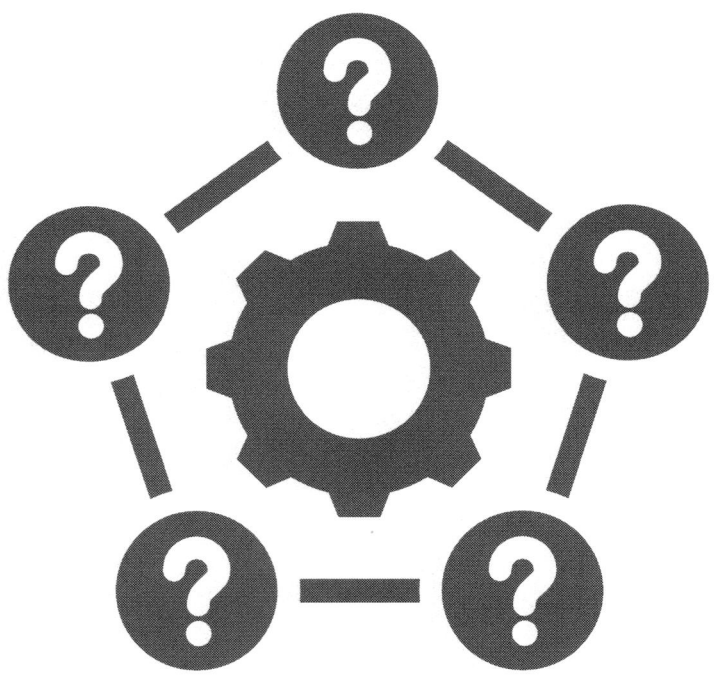

The 3 minute workbook

FIVE WHYS

Test your listening skills by asking someone something they like doing and ask why to five consecutive answers.

You will get to the root cause of their actions.

Why?

Next suggested workouts
11, 19, 22, 34, 35

Useful exercise to practice listening but also to enable expression of underlying motivation or inadequacy.

FREE WRITTING

The 3 minute workbook

FREE WRITING

Find a blank piece of paper, a pen and a quite spot.

Through free writing describe the colour 'yellow' to a blind person. The aim is to keep writing in flow for 3 minutes and not to erase what you have already scribed.

Consider what yellow may taste, smell, sound and feel like.

Why?

Next suggested workouts
7, 11, 36, 40

An useful way of learning how to articulate and express yourself.

GET IN THE ZONE

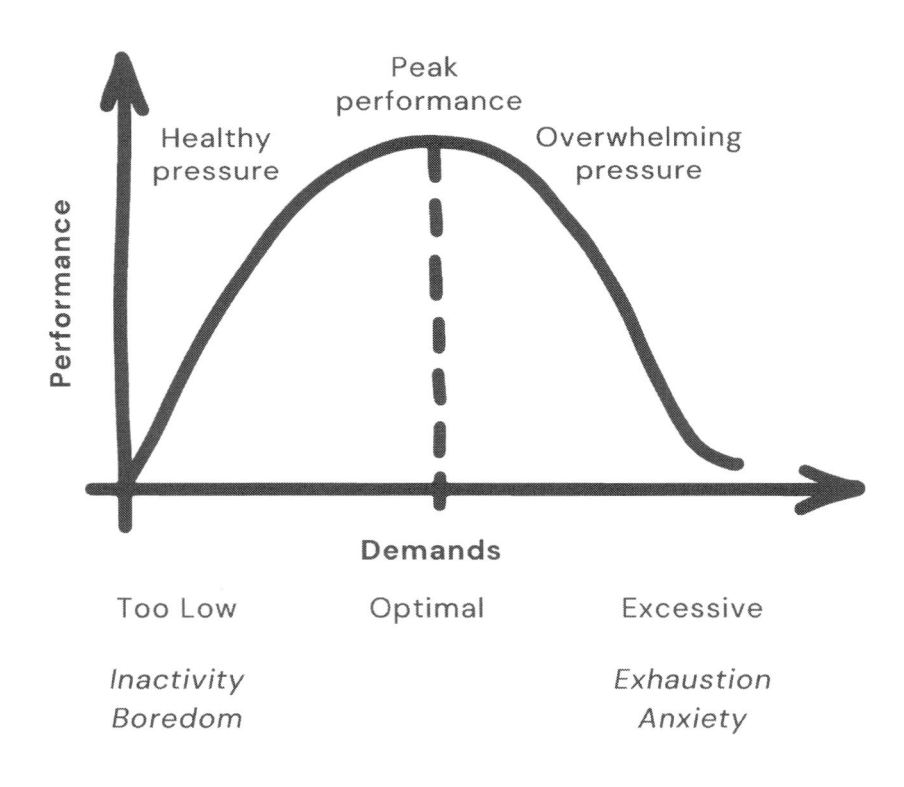

Performance (y-axis) vs **Demands** (x-axis)

- Healthy pressure
- Peak performance
- Overwhelming pressure

Too Low	Optimal	Excessive
Inactivity *Boredom*		*Exhaustion* *Anxiety*

Based on The Yerkes Dodson Law.

The 3 minute workbook

GET IN THE ZONE

Our performance improves, as pressure increases. But only up to a point.

Rate 1-10 (high) your 'stress' and 'performance' for up to 5 important areas of your life. Then, plot with an X on the Stress Performance curve. Review productivity and emotional impact implications for each X. Set boundaries to avoid burnout. Finally, review regularly.

Why?

Next suggested workouts
2, 34, 36, 41, 43

Visual way of appreciating the need and also potential drain from pressure.

INDEPENDENT OBSERVERS

QUALITY

RELEVANCE

IMPRESSION

The 3 minute workbook

INDEPENDENT OBSERVERS

Seek some objective opinions.

Invite a handful of diverse individuals who care about your work to rate the quality, perceived relevance and overall impression of a specific task, product or activity.

Why?

A useful and quick way to gain unbiased insight.

Next suggested workouts
9, 23, 34, 35, 40

INSIGHTFUL ARTIST

The 3 minute workbook

INSIGHTFUL ARTIST

Gather a blank paper and pencil.

Ask the participant to visualise an experience through a diagram and then to share their thinking.

Why?

Next suggested workouts
8, 19, 22, 28, 34

Useful to debunk assumptions and to understand how an individual perceives a given situation or place.

KINDNESS BINGO

The 3 minute workbook

KINDNESS BINGO

Think about when you are at your best and in service and aware of others.

Come up with up to 24 random acts of kindness.

Keep in sight and use your bingo card as often as possible to live your best and desired version.

Why?

Next suggested workouts
2, 11, 16, 20, 26

Helpful reference to experience, share and gain positivity from kindness.

LEADERSHIP STYLE

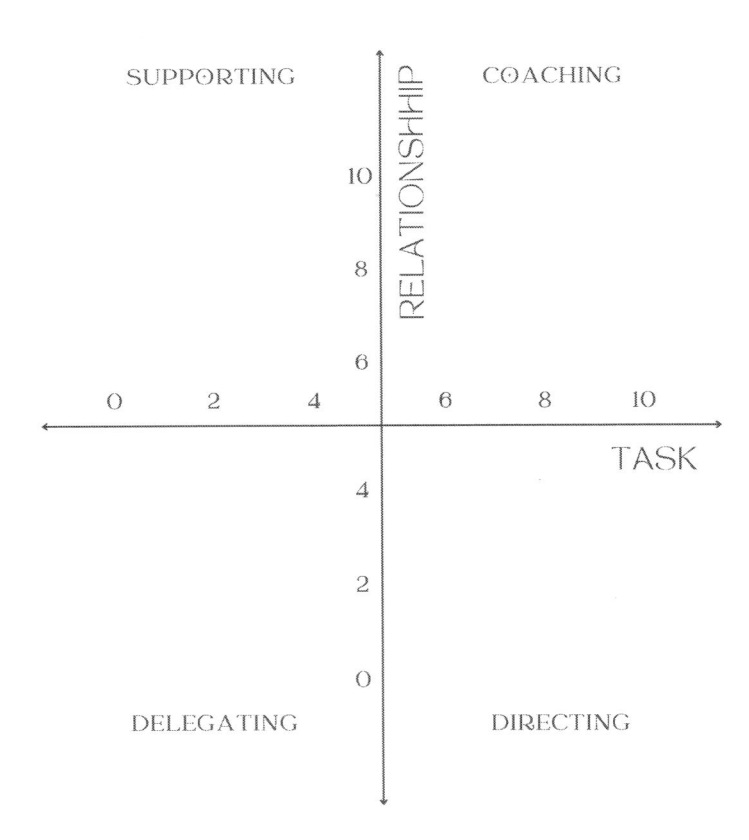

	RELATIONSHHIP	
SUPPORTING		COACHING
DELEGATING		DIRECTING

TASK

Attributed to Paul Heresy's situational leadership model.

LEADERSHIP STYLE

Read the seminal work by Paul Hersey on the situational leadership model (1961). Note how morale is shown to change with more or less support. Assess a colleagues relationship and task needs. Then, reflect on your leadership mix and adaptability.

Why?

Next suggested workouts
3, 25, 28, 34, 35

We all have different styles of behaviour. Hersey recognises that there is no one-size-fits-all approach. The leader, should change to be more or less directive, and more or less supportive, based on the situation.

LIFE MAP

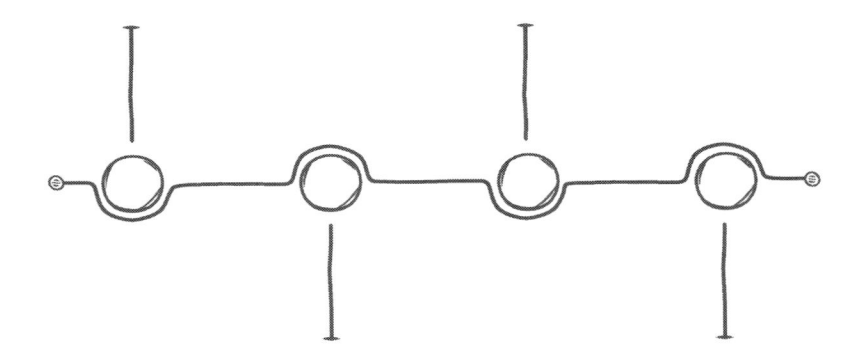

The 3 minute workbook

LIFE MAP

Every person goes through a change every year or so, from birth.

For every 2 years period of life, try to list at least 1 inflecting change. Start by recalling where you were. Write down all the good and worse moments. Take life as a novel or story by arranging these in a chronological timeline until the present day.

Next suggested workouts
1, 2, 25, 34, 40

Why?

Provides context of psychological effects of the past and to visualise desired moments in the future timeline.

LONG-RANGE FORECAST

The 3 minute workbook

LONG-RANGE FORECAST

Stay ahead.

Write up prose scenarios that describes how social and technological trends may influence your thoughts, behaviour, results and use or need of a particular product, service or environment.

Evaluate for changes you need to start making right now.

Why?

Next suggested workouts
2, 24, 34, 40, 41, 42

Quick way of constantly learning and innovating to keep on top of change.

NIRVANA LETTER

The 3 minute workbook

NIRVANA LETTER

Imagine yourself 10 years from now when your dreams and plans have come true.

Write a letter to someone you totally trust. Looking back and explain in great detail what you have done in the time between now and then. Deeply visualise the outcome. Be as vivid, specific, and reflective as possible.

Next suggested workouts
1, 25, 30, 35, 40, 43

Why?

A smart was to remove self-imposed restrictions because you act as if everything you've hoped for has already happened.

NOW WHAT

?

What, So What, Now What

A critical thinking model researched and developed by Rolfe et al.

The 3 minute workbook

NOW WHAT

Reflect. What have you or others tried, experienced or are experiencing.

So What happened or what does it means for you or others? Consider feelings, thoughts and effects on behaviour.

Now What will you do about what happened? Perhaps you want more or less of what happened.

Why?

Next suggested workouts
11, 22, 30, 34

A quick way helps move reflection into thinking and onto action.

NUDGE

The 3 minute workbook

NUDGE

Set an alarm on your phone at a regular time when you are normally awake, to repeat daily for 14 days.

The nudge is an invitation for you take a photo of where you are or of what you are experiencing at that exact moment. Narrative not required. Look back at your reel of photos and seek meaning and insights.

Why?

An insightful exploration into sub conscious decisions, routines and interactions.

Next suggested workouts
1, 2, 12, 25, 30

ODD DAY

The 3 minute workbook

ODD DAY

Your identity can be more than what you wear and what others see externally.

Have fun, be at your best, and celebrate difference and individuality by wearing something odd for a full day. Think odd hairclips, personal jewellery, socks, etc.

Why?

Build confidence and appreciation for you while having fun.

Next suggested workouts
2, 11, 14, 34

PASSION DRIVERS

SELF BELIEF

OPTIMISM

FREEDOM

A coaching framework adapted by Kartik Bharadia.

The 3 minute workbook

PASSION DRIVERS

List 5 ways to influence and evoke positive emotions in an environment, team or individual that you are connected with.

Specifically consider how to promote the 3 passion drivers: freedom, optimism and self belief.

Now implement your list.

Why?

Next suggested workouts
8, 13, 28, 30, 32, 34

Useful strategy to bring forth personality and urgency.

PITCH MATRIX

WHY THIS PROBLEM?	**WHY THIS SOLUTION?**
WHY NOW?	**WHY YOU?**

The 3 minute workbook

PITCH MATRIX

New ideas come to us or are pitched to us constantly. Often we choose one over the other.

Think of a project or idea you are considering or have recently taken on. Then ask yourself, what is the depth and frequency of the problem. Why is your solution appropriate? What is the consequence of inaction? Why are you uniquely suited to the solution?

Why?

Next suggested workouts
8, 12, 27, 30, 38, 41, 42

Useful to validate projects that are mentally, time or financially intensive.

PREDICT A HEADLINE

The 3 minute workbook

PREDICT A HEADLINE

This is an invitation to predict into the future.

Identify what you want to be famous for. Write down the headline. Picture the supporting imagery vividly.

Now, think about how you want to get there and the changes required.

Why?

Next suggested workouts
2, 3, 5, 12, 23, 30, 32, 42

Useful exercise to envision a bold goal to pursue.

PROJECTIONS

The 3 minute workbook

PROJECTIONS

Write down 10 attributes of an effective leader, each on separate cards. Note down 4 from this pack that you exhibit most when working in a productive and healthy state.

Using the 10 cards, ask a handful of trusted people to pick out 4 qualities that they think you champion most often and contrast against your selection.

Why?

Self awareness is a two sided coin, being aware is one and knowing how you project yourself is another.

Next suggested workouts
3, 12, 14, 15, 19, 34, 41

REGULATE. RELATE. REASON

Attributed to Bruce Perry.

The 3 minute workbook

REGULATE, RELATE, REASON

Think of a moment you experienced a child or an adult experiencing a meltdown. They seem inconsolable.

Reflect on how you could have used the 3 R's model to manage the situation. Regulate their stress hormones by calming them. Relate to their needs or loss. To reason, use story to access higher level thinking and share any lessons for both sides.

Why?

Next suggested workouts
3, 5, 7, 9, 11, 32,

Useful to help others to self regulate in stressful situations. A bottom-up approach building up to the reasoning.

REVERSE THINKING

The 3 minute workbook

REVERSE THINKING

Think and record 3 worst-case scenarios of a goal you are working toward.

Now take control. Use this account to discover what to do and your options to make sure this does not happen.

Why?

Useful exercise to prevent worst-case scenario but also to identify the obvious things that should be done correclty and consitently.

Next suggested workouts
6, 8, 23, 30, 33, 35, 42

SCALING

★★★★½

The 3 minute workbook

SCALING

Identify a task or a process and ask the team to rate themselves on a scale of 1-10 (10 = can complete the action independently without support, 1 = highly dependent).

Evaluate support or actions required.

Why?

Quantitative and effective way of measuring confidence of the team and where to channel energy toward. Scaling can also be used to measure will, importance, experience or perceptions.

Next suggested workouts
9, 11, 19, 30, 41, 42

SCREENPLAY

The 3 minute workbook

SCREENPLAY

Think of a difficult conversation you should be having with someone you know and interact with. Write a script between you and the other individual. Jot down words of your opening statement and how they react and reply in their words. Each time type your response to theirs. Repeat this back and forth dialogue for up to 5 responses each. Finally, evaluate to see if you would like to change any of your statements to change the reply.

Why?

Useful to build empathy and emotional understanding of both sides.

Next suggested workouts
3, 4, 8, 7, 11, 34

SELF APPRAISAL MATRIX

WHAT ARE YOUR MOST SIGNIFICANT ACCOMPLISHMENTS SINCE YOUR LAST SELF-APPRAISAL?	WHAT ARE THE MOST IMPORTANT THINGS YOU WILL FOCUS ON BEFORE YOUR NEXT REVIEW?
WHAT OBSTACLES ARE YOU ENCOUNTERING RIGHT NOW?	WHAT CAN OTHERS BETTER OR DIFFERENTLY TO SUPPORT YOU? ANY OTHER LOCAL OPPORTUNITIES?

☐ DATE/TIME _____ ☐ DATE/TIME _____

☐ DATE/TIME _____ ☐ DATE/TIME _____

The 3 minute workbook

SELF APPRAISAL MATRIX

Agree regular catch up sessions with yourself. Think date and time. Track your completion.

Type up your self appraisal before each session and review the previous self appraisal matrix for insights.

Why?

Next suggested workouts
1, 32, 33, 34, 43

The insightful technique to appreciate progress. focus on key priorities and opportunities. On the other had you can foresee and overcome obstacles.

SOCIAL COGNITIVE THEORY

Albert Bandura's earlier bobo doll experiments in 1961 inspired the social cognitive theory (1976).

The 3 minute workbook

SOCIAL COGNITIVE THEORY

This model suggests that individuals can learn from simply observing others and develop self-beliefs that influence their behaviour.

Observe a mentor, role-model or a highly effective colleague doing their work without interference.

Why?

Next suggested workouts
22, 25, 33, 34, 41, 42

The learning process follows three phases attention, retention, and behavioural reproduction and is not dependant on a formal teacher. As long as learning capacity and motivation exist.

STATE MANAGEMENT

Result

↑

Behaviour

↑

State

The 3 minute workbook

STATE MANAGEMENT

When you are in a happy state, if someone did something to anger you, you could centre your emotions and your reaction. In an angry state, the same situation can cause irritation.

Ask yourself, in your desired state how do you feel, think, behave. What do you see, hear and taste. Note this state and create it often.

Why?

Next suggested workouts
11, 14, 25, 36, 43

Give yourself the space to see new, more positive, and healthier meanings to situations, yourself, or others.

SWOT MATRIX

STRENGTHS

What unique strengths do you have?

What do others see as your strengths?

WEAKNESSES

What could you do better?

What do others see as your weaknesses?

OPPORTUNITIES

What strengths could you turn into opportunities?

What local opportunities can you seize?

THREATS

What changes or weaknesses could expose you?

What obstacles can you foresee?

Originally known as SOFT Analysis is attributed to Albert Humphrey.

The 3 minute workbook

SWOT MATRIX

Evaluate your strong and weak points.

Start by looking at the internal strengths and weaknesses, and then build on those to evaluate the more external opportunities and threats.

Finally, take action to maximise the strengths and opportunities and minimise the weaknesses and threats.

Why?

Next suggested workouts
12, 16, 19, 25, 34

An efficient tool to evaluate an individuals career plan. Traditionally used by businesses for go to market strategising.

TGROW

A coaching framework by Myles Downey, Effective coaching (2003). Adapted from the GROW model by by Whitmore, Fine and Alexander.

The 3 minute workbook

TGROW

Think about one specific Topic or challenge you are working on. In the long term, what is your Goal related to this issue?

What do you see as the Real issue here? What have you done so far?

What Options would move you forward just one step? What is your Will on a 1-10 scale to take action?

Why?

Next suggested workouts
11, 12, 19, 23, 30, 41

A useful and guided excercise to clarify a topic, the issues and to measure commitement.

THE SMART MODEL

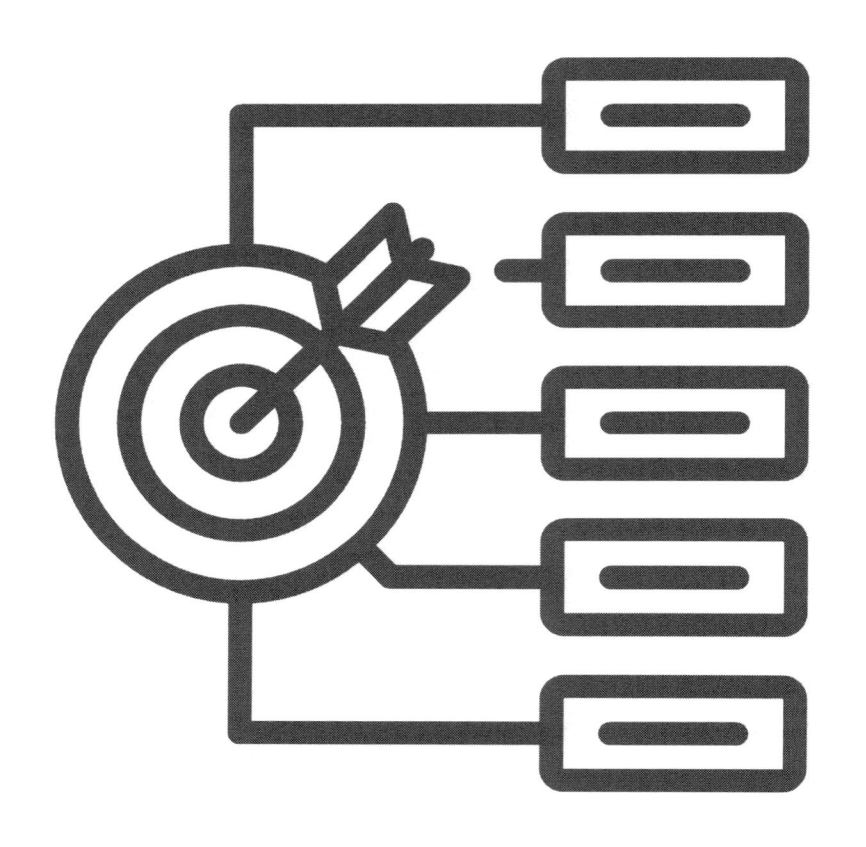

Developed by G Doran, A Miller and J Cunningham in 1981.

THE SMART MODEL

Use your time and resources productively by writing down a Specific, Measurable, Achievable, Relevant and Time-bound goal for a passionate focus at present.

Then, evaluate your plan.

Why?
Useful exercise to make sure goals are clear and reachable.

Next suggested workouts
2, 3, 5, 12, 23, 30, 32

THE 4 7 8 4

The 3 minute workbook

THE 4 7 8 4

The 4-7-8 breathing technique involves breathing in for 4 seconds, holding the breath for 7 seconds, and exhaling for 8 seconds.

Without a break, repeat the entire technique 4 times in a row.

Why?

Next suggested workouts
1, 8, 11, 14, 19, 32

A practical way for highly active people to reduce anxiety or get to sleep.

TIME-LAPSE VIDEO

The 3 minute workbook

TIME-LAPSE VIDEO

Take a longitudinal perspective through a new lens.

Set up a time-lapse video to elicit your movements in a space you regularly take energy from.

Then, evaluate.

Why?

Next suggested workouts
11, 12, 14, 20, 24, 36, 41, 43

Useful to self evaluate productivity, operations and interactions.

USER STORY

The 3 minute workbook

USER STORY

To write well is to think clearly.

Write a story of how you positively impacted someone else or something near you. Describe in detail the story of the past and how things were before your input and the pain you healed or everted.

Then, share a vision and potential of how many more lives could be transformed with a similar focus.

Why?

Next suggested workouts
3, 6, 23, 24, 33, 34

Stories can be transformational if we recall the empowering ones.

VIEW IT AGAIN

The 3 minute workbook

VIEW IT AGAIN

Draw the same object or scene, like a coffee mug or a street scene, every day for a week.

See what new details or nuances you notice as you examine the object or scene every day.

Why?

Next suggested workouts
5, 32, 37, 42

Extreme focus like this should improve your attention to detail and help you notice new elements in your work.

VISION BOARD

The 3 minute workbook

VISION BOARD

Immerse yourself in a visual representation of what you want or hope to achieve.

Set up to 5 goals for the future. Then, add visually inspiring images, cut outs, and quotes linked to your goals.

Create an inspiring composition of everything, which will motivate you daily when you look at it. Finally, add positive affirmations or annotations.

Next suggested workouts
1, 2, 3, 5, 12, 23, 30, 32, 43

Why?

A proven way to focus daily and think of new ways to achieve your goals.

WHEEL OF WORK

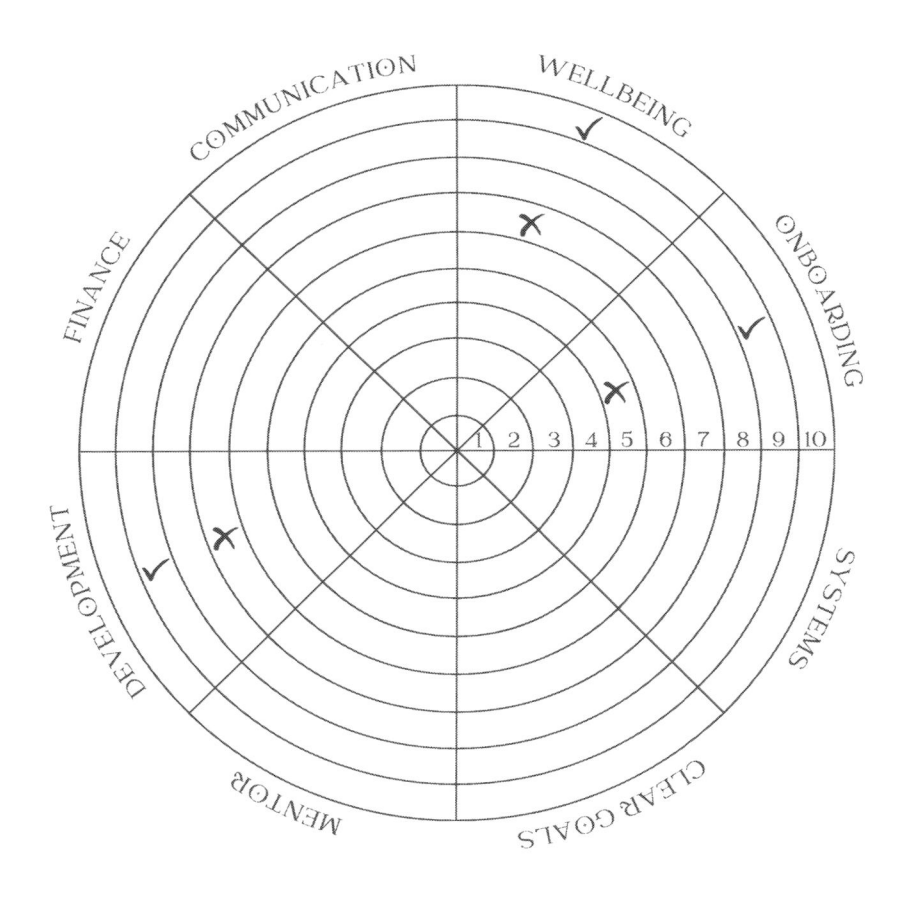

A concept originally created by Paul J. Meyer.

The 3 minute workbook

WHEEL OF WORK

The wheel of work is a visualisation tool that helps you better channel your time. List 8 live priorities that contribute toward your success at work. Then, rate how much time you devote to each 1 – 10 (high). Now, rate each again 1 – 10 (high), for what would be the ideal time to devote. Finally, commit to plan for up to 3 areas to close the gap current vs desired time.

Why?

Next suggested workouts
2, 8, 11, 19, 23, 25, 34, 35,

Different areas of your work will need different levels of attention at different times.

ZERO DRAFT

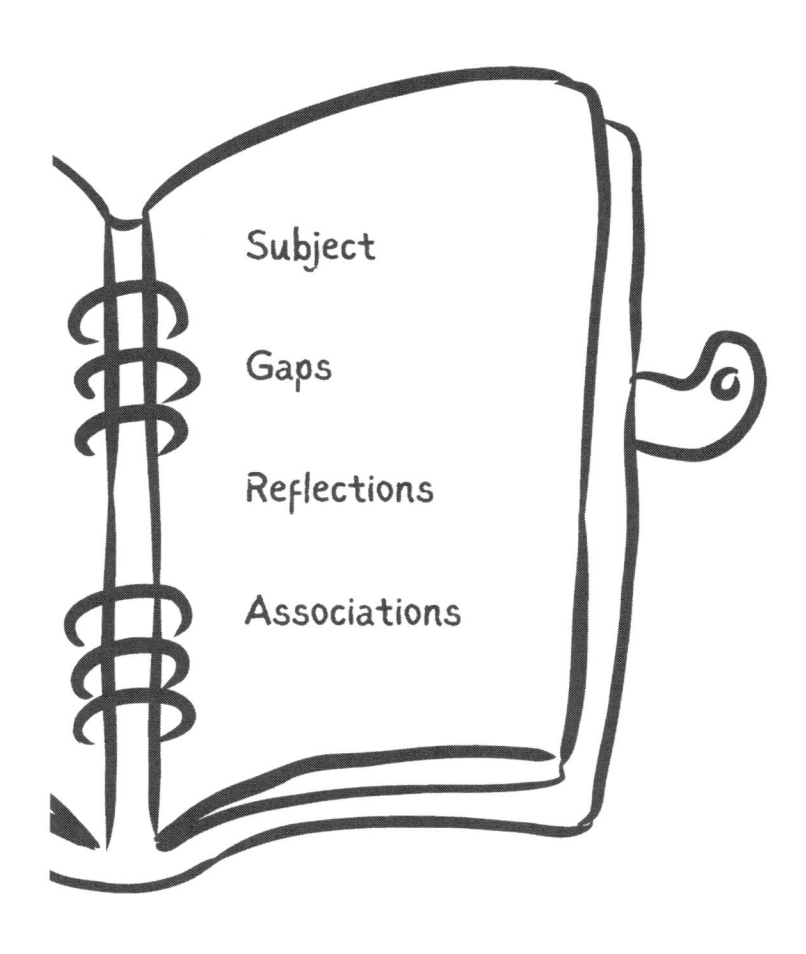

Subject

Gaps

Reflections

Associations

The 3 minute workbook

ZERO DRAFT

Start an idea from scratch that you are excited about.

Write down everything you know about the subject you are interested in, then everything you want to know about a topic, a reflection of why this is important to you and finally jot down anything else that came to mind.

Why?

Next suggested workouts
3, 5, 12, 23, 30, 32, 33, 41

Useful exercise to gain clarity of the idea, resources required and your core motivations that will keep you going through the toughest of times.

3 MINUTE JOURNAL

DATE   /   /

WHAT I'M GRATEFUL FOR

- *Something near me, an inspiration, someone, an event*

-

SOMETHING NEW TODAY

- *An activity, experiment, learning*

-

GOALS OR AMBITIONS

-

-

ACCOMPLISHMENTS

-

-

WHAT CAN BE IMPROVED

-

-

ACTIONS

-

-

FREE THOUGHTS

_____
_____
_____
_____
_____
_____
_____

The 3 minute workbook

3 MINUTE JOURNAL

If you have got this far in the coaching workbook you will want to focus on your thoughts, goals, feelings, behaviours and achievements.

Enter journal entries for the next 14 days. You can use the 3 minute journal template provided on the opposite page to kickstart the process.

Why?

Next suggested workouts
1, 2, 9, 11, 12, 14, 23, 30, 35, 36, 40, 42

A low demand and high challenge routine to create order. Get to know yourself by revealing your most private fears, thoughts, and feelings.

☐ GRATITUDE ☐ KPIS/ GOALS ☐ IMPROVEMENTS
☐ EXPERIMENTS ☐ ACHIEVEMENTS ☐ ACTIONS

The 3 minute workbook

☐ GRATITUDE ☐ KPIS/ GOALS ☐ IMPROVEMENTS

☐ EXPERIMENTS ☐ ACHIEVEMENTS ☐ ACTIONS

☐ GRATITUDE ☐ KPIS/ GOALS ☐ IMPROVEMENTS
☐ EXPERIMENTS ☐ ACHIEVEMENTS ☐ ACTIONS

The 3 minute workbook

☐ GRATITUDE ☐ KPIS/ GOALS ☐ IMPROVEMENTS

☐ EXPERIMENTS ☐ ACHIEVEMENTS ☐ ACTIONS

☐ GRATITUDE   ☐ KPIS/ GOALS   ☐ IMPROVEMENTS

☐ EXPERIMENTS ☐ ACHIEVEMENTS   ☐ ACTIONS

The 3 minute workbook

- [ ] GRATITUDE - [ ] KPIS/ GOALS - [ ] IMPROVEMENTS
- [ ] EXPERIMENTS - [ ] ACHIEVEMENTS - [ ] ACTIONS

☐ GRATITUDE   ☐ KPIS/ GOALS   ☐ IMPROVEMENTS
☐ EXPERIMENTS   ☐ ACHIEVEMENTS   ☐ ACTIONS

The 3 minute workbook

☐ GRATITUDE ☐ KPIS/ GOALS ☐ IMPROVEMENTS
☐ EXPERIMENTS ☐ ACHIEVEMENTS ☐ ACTIONS

☐ GRATITUDE ☐ KPIS/ GOALS ☐ IMPROVEMENTS

☐ EXPERIMENTS ☐ ACHIEVEMENTS ☐ ACTIONS

The 3 minute workbook

☐ GRATITUDE ☐ KPIS/ GOALS ☐ IMPROVEMENTS
☐ EXPERIMENTS ☐ ACHIEVEMENTS ☐ ACTIONS

	GRATITUDE		KPIS/ GOALS		IMPROVEMENTS
	EXPERIMENTS		ACHIEVEMENTS		ACTIONS

The 3 minute workbook

☐ GRATITUDE ☐ KPIS/ GOALS ☐ IMPROVEMENTS
☐ EXPERIMENTS ☐ ACHIEVEMENTS ☐ ACTIONS

☐ GRATITUDE ☐ KPIS/ GOALS ☐ IMPROVEMENTS
☐ EXPERIMENTS ☐ ACHIEVEMENTS ☐ ACTIONS

The 3 minute workbook

☐ GRATITUDE ☐ KPIS/ GOALS ☐ IMPROVEMENTS
☐ EXPERIMENTS ☐ ACHIEVEMENTS ☐ ACTIONS

The 3 minute workbook

NOTES

The 3 minute workbook

The 3 minute workbook

The 3 minute workbook

The 3 minute workbook

The 3 minute workbook

AUTHOR

KARTIK BHARADIA has led frontline teams from the age of nineteen years. Since then, influencing a diverse range of colleagues and clients on a daily basis was a necessity.

He delivers in person workshops on leadership, skills and commercial awareness. Kartik learnt to face his limiting beliefs and challenging situations with colleagues who had been in roles longer than him or more often than not, senior in age. What he shares is a mix of knowledge from mentors, lessons from mistakes and importantly references to timeless academically critiqued models.

www.kartikbharadia.com

What made this workbook

- Recruiting and leading teams of 30+ direct reports
- Proprietorship and operations of a service based business with 1000+ customers/ month
- Education and practical application of coaching
- Corporate leadership, skills and commercial training

The 3 minute workbook

Printed in Great Britain
by Amazon